D1441982

WORLD WAR II CHRONICLES

THE RISE OF JAPAN AND PEARL HARBOR

DWIGHT JON ZIMMERMAN,
MILITARY HISTORY CONSULTANT

BY JULIE KLAM

Published by Smart Apple Media, 1980 Lookout Drive, North Mankato, Minnesota 56003

Produced by Byron Preiss Visual Publications, Inc.

Library of Congress Cataloging-in-Publication Data

Klam, Julie.

The rise of Japan and Pearl Harbor / by Julie Klam.

v. cm. — (World War II chronicles; bk. 2)

Contents: Rise of military government in Japan — Japanese atrocities in China — U.S. vs. Japan: the diplomatic war part 1 — FDR's fireside chats — U.S. vs. Japan: the diplomatic war part 2 — Pearl Harbor — The Japanese tide of conquest — The sinking of the HMS *Repulse* and HMS *Prince of Wales* — The surrender of Singapore — The Battle of the Java Sea — America's top commanders — Battle of the Coral Sea — The China-Burma-India theater — Battle of Midway.

ISBN 1-58340-188-1

1. Pearl Harbor (Hawaii), Attack on, 1941—Juvenile literature. 2. Japan—History—1926-1945—Juvenile literature. 3. World War, 1939-1945—Causes—Juvenile literature. 4. World War, 1939-1945—Pacific Ocean—Juvenile literature. [1. Pearl Harbor (Hawaii), Attack on, 1941. 2. Japan—History—1926-1945. 3. World War, 1939-1945—Causes. 4. World War, 1939-1945—Pacific Ocean.] I. Title.

D767 .K538 2002

940.54'26—dc21   2002017646

First Edition

2 4 6 8 9 7 5 3 1

CONTENTS:

INTRODUCTION

✝ (opposite): Adolf Hitler addresses the Reichstag.

World War II was the greatest conflict of the 20th century. Fought on every continent except Antarctica and across every ocean, it was truly a "world war." Like many other wars, over time it evolved. Modern technology and strategic advancements changed the rules of combat forever, allowing for widespread attacks from the air, the ground, and the sea.

For the Chinese, the war began in 1931, when Japan invaded northeastern China. When Germany invaded Poland in 1939, Europeans were dragged into the fray. Americans did not enter World War II until December 7, 1941, when Japan attacked Pearl Harbor, Hawaii.

World War II pitted two sides against each other, the Axis powers and the Allied countries. The main Axis nations were Germany, Japan, and Italy. The Axis powers were led by Chancellor Adolf Hitler, the head of the Nazi Party in Germany; Premier Benito Mussolini, the head of the Fascists in Italy; and Japan's Emperor Hirohito and the military government headed by Prime Minister Hideki Tojo. The Allies included Britain, France, the Soviet Union, China, and the United States. The leaders of the Allies were Britain's Prime

✝ Benito Mussolini

✝ Hirohito

Minister Winston Churchill, who had replaced Neville Chamberlain in 1940; General Charles de Gaulle of France; the Soviet Union's Marshal Josef Stalin; China's Generalissimo Chiang Kai-shek; and Franklin Delano Roosevelt, the president of the United States. The two sides clashed primarily in the Pacific Ocean and Asia, which Japan sought to control, and in the Atlantic Ocean, Europe, and North Africa, where Germany and Italy were trying to take over.

World War II finally ended in 1945, first in Europe on May 8, with Germany's total capitulation. Then, on September 2, the Japanese signed the document for their unconditional surrender after the United States had dropped two atomic bombs on Japan. World War II left 50 million people dead and millions of others wounded, both physically and mentally.

The war encompassed the feats of extraordinary heroes and the worst villains imaginable, with thrilling triumphs and heartrending tragedies. *The Rise of Japan and Pearl Harbor* covers the events that led to the war in the Pacific and continues through the bombing of Pearl Harbor. The book culminates with the first Allied victory, at the Battle of Midway.

✝ Charles de Gaulle

✝ Josef Stalin

✝ Chiang Kai-shek

✝ (right): Franklin Delano Roosevelt

Map of German Conquests

- Germany (1939)
- Axis Occupied Territory (1942)
- Italy and Its Territories
- Treaty with Axis
- Allied Powers
- Allied Protectorates
- Neutral Countries
- Vichy France and Territories

NORWAY

FINLAND

SWEDEN

North Sea

ESTONIA

NORWAY

Baltic Sea

LATVIA

IRELAND

UNITED KINGDOM

DENMARK

LITHUANIA

UNION OF SOVIET SOCIALIST REPUBLICS

EAST PRUSSIA

THE NETHERLANDS

Atlantic Ocean

BELGIUM

GERMANY

POLAND

LUXEMBOURG

FRANCE

SLOVAKIA

SWITZERLAND

HUNGARY

VICHY FRANCE

ROMANIA

Black Sea

YUGOSLAVIA

Adriatic Sea

PORTUGAL

SPAIN

ITALY

BULGARIA

ALBANIA

TURKEY

GREECE

SYRIA

SPANISH MOROCCO

IRAQ

Mediterranean Sea

PALESTINE

MOROCCO

TRANS-JORDAN

TUNISIA

ALGERIA

EGYPT

SAUDI ARABIA

LIBYA

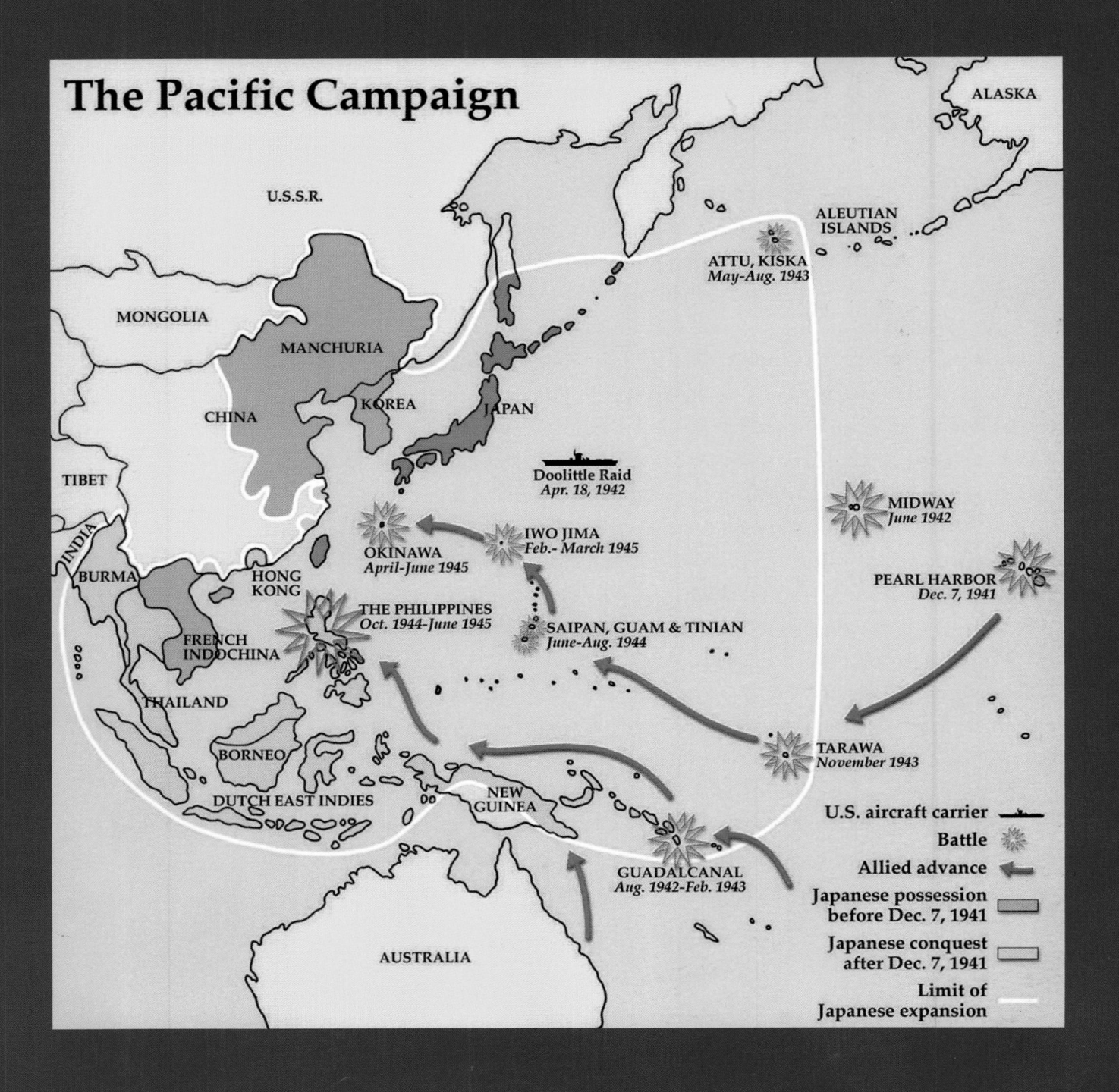

THE RISE OF MILITARY GOVERNMENT IN JAPAN

In World War I (1914–18), Japan and Italy fought on the side of the Allies—Great Britain, France, the United States, and Russia—against Germany, Austria-Hungary, and the Ottoman Empire, called the Central Powers. In World War II, Japan sided with Germany and Italy to fight Great Britain, France, and the United States. This dramatic change had its origin in the conference to draw up the peace treaty to end World War I, the Treaty of Versailles.

Although Japan fought on the side of the victorious Allies in World War I, it was not included with Great Britain, France, the United States, and Italy (known as the Big Four) as part of the primary negotiating group for the Treaty of Versailles, which formally settled the peace terms of World War I. Rather, Japan was grouped in what was called the Council of Ten, nations who sided with the Allies or benefited from the Allies' victory and would be consulted on a provisional basis.

When the Treaty of Versailles was finally signed in 1919, Japan was unhappy and frustrated. The Japanese felt that they did not receive proper territorial gains, and they were angry at what they felt was the condescending treatment their delegates received at the conference.

At the conclusion of World War I, Japan had become a major power in Asia. But, as was the case with other nations, the worldwide economic collapse in the 1930s—the Great Depression—weakened that power. Declining exports and a troubled economy produced the same

 The 1919 Peace Conference at Versailles, France.

unrest that was bubbling in many other parts of the globe, and Japan's citizens blamed their government. They saw the Western-style democracy that ruled in Japan as too soft in defending the country's economic interests. Japanese nationalists, people who were strongly pro-Japan and anti-Western, criticized the government for a series of diplomatic setbacks. These included Britain's refusal to renew its treaty of alliance with Japan; a series of U.S. legislative acts that restricted Japanese immigration; Britain's construction of a naval base in Singapore (seen by Japan as a direct challenge to its power); and the Washington Naval Conference Treaty, a naval limitation treaty that forced Japan to accept an inferior ratio of capital ship construction compared to that of the United States and Britain. These setbacks offended Japanese pride.

During the 1930s, Japan's parliamentary democracy gave way to nationalist and militarist control. By the middle of the decade, Japan's government was composed of a number of competing special interest groups, with the army having the most influence. Many political enemies who opposed the military government were persecuted or assassinated. Pro-military propaganda, like that in Germany and Italy, filled the media. Prince Fumimaro Konoe was prime minister, and many important government posts were held by army or navy officers.

Between 1936 and 1941, the Japanese military grew by quantum leaps. By 1940, the Japanese navy was stronger than the combined navies of the United States and Britain in the Pacific. It had 300,000 troops and another two million reservists. Japan's primary industry was war production, and clearly this was no longer simply defensive.

⊦ The World Disarmament Conference in
 Washington, D.C., November 21, 1921.

JAPANESE ATROCITIES IN CHINA

Japan's growth as a modern military power began just before the turn of the 20th century. At that time, there were two nations that could challenge its rising role as a major power in Asia: Russia and China.

Japan defeated Russia in the Russo-Japanese war of 1904–05. After that, only China remained to challenge Japan. Japan made its first big move against China when in 1931 it annexed Manchuria, a Chinese province that had been historically disputed between Russia, Japan, and China. The Japanese changed the province's name to Manchukou. The League of Nations (a multinational organization like today's United Nations but with fewer members and a lot less power) criticized Japan's actions. Japan, a member, responded by leaving the League. Japan soon after tore up the Washington Naval Conference Treaty.

On July 7, 1937—the date considered by many to be the real start of World War II—the "China Incident" on the Marco Polo Bridge near Peking (modern-day Beijing) occurred when shots were fired on Japanese troops. This was

CHINA'S CIVIL WAR

It is important to understand that since the 1920s China had been involved in a civil war between the Nationalist Party, led by Generalissimo Chiang Kai-shek, and the Chinese Communist Party, led by Mao Tse-tung (now known as Mao Zedong). Even after Japan attacked China, the two groups continued to fight each other, though not as often.

In 1949, the Chinese Communists successfully drove the Nationalists out of China, forcing them to flee to the island of Formosa (later called Taiwan), where they created the Republic of China.

✠ A terrified baby after a 1937 Japanese air attack on Shanghai, China.

A meeting of the Lytton Commission, which was appointed by the League of Nations to investigate the Manchurian Incident, September 1932.

the excuse Japan used to justify its invasion of China. One of the Japanese targets was the Nationalist capital of Nanking. Japanese bombs decimated the city and destroyed more than half the buildings, but that was only the beginning. When the troops captured the city in December 1937, they committed a series of heinous atrocities that came to be known as the "Rape of Nanking." Before it ended, more than 300,000 people were murdered, and an estimated 80,000 Chinese women were raped.

Despite this and other devastating attacks, Japan was never able to conquer China. Even so, by 1940, Japan felt strong enough to create a plan for Japanese domination in Asia: the Greater East Asia Co-Prosperity Sphere.

THE U.S. VS. JAPAN: THE DIPLOMATIC WAR PART 1

In December 1937, while Japan waged war against China, it also bombed and sunk the American gunboat *Panay*. Japan called the bombing an accident and apologized to the United States, though there was great doubt that the attack was not pre-planned. The United States wrote off the incident without retribution, and the Japanese interpreted its response as weak. Japan would be even less hesitant to be aggressive toward the United States later.

International tensions increased as Japan occupied the territory of French Indochina (Cambodia, Laos, and Vietnam). It now had

⊬ The American gunboat *Panay*.

+ Roosevelt gives a speech in October 1937 condemning the invasions of Ethiopia and China.

possession of naval and air bases from Saigon to Hanoi. The Japanese could now threaten the British military base in Singapore, the U.S. military bases in the Philippines, and the oil-rich Dutch East Indies. Their goal of the complete domination of Asia was now in sight.

President Roosevelt was in an awkward situation. Officially, the United States was neutral. Also, isolationists were very powerful in the United States, and they were determined to keep the country out of any conflict. But Roosevelt saw that Japan's ongoing actions were morally wrong and, sooner or later, would threaten the United States. Initially, he used words and then economic sanctions that stopped U.S. companies from selling oil, iron, and other raw materials to Japan. Thus the seeds of conflict were planted.

In September 1940, Japan signed the mutual defense agreement called the Tripartite Pact with the Pact of Steel members, Germany and Italy. Mussolini called them the "Axis" nations to describe the common goals of Fascist Italy, Nazi Germany, and Imperialist Japan. Japan also signed a separate non-aggression pact with the Soviet Union the following year. The Japanese believed that these measures would cause the United States, the only country that by 1940 was powerful enough to pose a threat, to think twice before interfering with Japan's conquests.

> ## MEANWHILE IN EUROPE
>
> In March 1938, German Chancellor Adolf Hitler announces the "Anschluss" (union) with Austria, thus making that country a state within Germany.

PRESIDENT ROOSEVELT'S FIRESIDE CHATS

As it became increasingly clear to President Roosevelt that the United States might have to enter the war, he knew he would need to rally the isolationists, those Americans who wanted to stay out of the war.

Roosevelt was an engaging and inspiring speaker. He artfully used the popular medium of radio to send out the messages he needed the American public to receive in his Fireside Chats. Two particularly important chats got public opinion heavily on FDR's (Franklin Delano Roosevelt) side.

On December 29, 1940, Roosevelt gave his "Arsenal of Democracy" speech. In it, he outlined the effects of the Tripartite Pact that Japan, Italy, and Germany had signed with one another and the looming threat to the U.S. Navy in the Pacific. He explained that the world had learned lessons about the Nazis, that "no nation can appease the Nazis. No man can tame a tiger into a kitten by stroking it."

Roosevelt railed against "American appeasers," calling them accomplices to the Axis powers. He told of the need to "increase our production of all the implements of defense." Roosevelt said he believed that the Axis nations would lose the war, but only if the American people could be more determined in their efforts than they had ever been before. He said:

We must be the great arsenal of democracy. For us this is an emergency as serious as war itself. We must apply ourselves to our

⊦ President Roosevelt delivers one of his Fireside Chat speeches over the radio.

task with the same resolution, the same sense of urgency, the same spirit of patriotism and sacrifice as we would show were we at war.

A week later, on January 6, 1941, Roosevelt followed up with his State of the Union address, the "Four Freedoms" speech. He warned:

The future and the safety of our country and of our democracy are overwhelmingly involved in events far beyond our borders.

He said that the United States would have to continue the building of defense to ensure Americans' safety and that all national resources, and higher taxes, should go toward combating this "foreign peril." He outlined the Lend-Lease Act. The act said that the United States would lend arms to other nations, rather than selling them, and those nations would give them back after the war.

Roosevelt's conclusion was meant to rally every American to the cause:

In the future days, which we seek to make secure, we look forward to a world founded upon four essential

This is America..

...where a mighty nation is devoting its total power to defend the four freedoms - - freedom of speech, freedom of worship, freedom from want, freedom from fear ★ This is your America

... Keep it Free!

⊬ A World War II-era "Four Freedoms" poster.

human freedoms. The first is freedom of speech and expression—everywhere in the world. The second is freedom of every person to worship God in his own way— everywhere in the world. The third is freedom from want—which, translated into world terms, means economic understandings which will secure to every nation a healthy peacetime life for its inhabitants—everywhere in the world.

The fourth is freedom from fear—which, translated into world terms, means a worldwide reduction of armaments to such a point and in such a thorough fashion that no nation will be in a position to commit an act of physical aggression against any neighbor—anywhere in the world.

Japan felt it had won the diplomatic war it had been waging with the United States when it signed the Tripartite Pact and the non-aggression treaty with the Soviet Union in 1940. But President Roosevelt refused to be intimidated. Instead, he said that the United States would take any and all steps necessary to oppose Japanese aggression. Because of the isolationist sentiment, these steps had to be diplomatic, but they would still be very powerful.

Roosevelt, supported by the British and the Dutch, froze Japanese assets and cut off oil shipments to the country. Now Japan would not have the oil and steel crucial for its war machine. Japan had hoped America would do anything to avoid fighting it in the Pacific and the Nazis in the Atlantic; now it realized this was not the case. Japan would either have to pull out of China and Indochina or go to war with the United States.

From August to November 1941, Japan tried to reach an acceptable political compromise with the United States. Japan outlined its demands. Japan wanted the Americans "to not meddle in or interrupt" its actions in China and stop supporting the Chinese. It also wanted to be allowed to stay in French Indochina and did not want any reinforcements of American air bases in the Far East. In addition, Japan wanted the United States to resume commercial relations with it. Granting these demands would have been a humiliating diplomatic defeat to the United States, and America made

"I am looking forward to dictating peace to the United States in the White House at Washington"
— ADMIRAL YAMAMOTO

What do YOU say, AMERICA?

✛ An American propaganda poster features Admiral Yamamoto, the man who planned the attack on Pearl Harbor.

it clear that none of the demands would be met.

The impasse was complicated by the fact that in October 1941, the Japanese military forced Prime Minister Konoe, who genuinely wanted peace, to resign. His successor, General Tojo, ordered the negotiations to continue. But the talks were a smoke screen to hide the fact that Japan had ordered its fleet to attack Pearl Harbor, Hawaii, home of the U.S. Pacific fleet.

On December 6, 1941, American intelligence intercepted a note from the Japanese government to its ambassadors in the United States. The note instructed the ambassadors to break diplomatic relations with the United States and provided instructions to destroy code machines in the Japanese embassy. American intelligence and Japanese ambassadors all understood what this meant. War was about to be declared.

The United States sent warnings to American commanders in Hawaii, the Philippines, Panama, and San Francisco. Because of difficulty with communications in Hawaii, the message went by commercial telegraph. It would reach Lieutenant General Walter C. Short, commander of U.S. Army forces in Hawaii, and Admiral Husband E. Kimmel, commander of the Pacific fleet, on December 7, 1941, at about 3:00 P.M.—seven hours after the Japanese attack had started.

MEANWHILE IN EUROPE

In August 1941, President Roosevelt and British Prime Minister Winston Churchill announce the Atlantic Charter, and the German army begins its siege of Leningrad. In September 1941, Nazis begin using gas chambers in the Auschwitz concentration camp. In October 1941, the German army begins its advance on Moscow.

In the early morning of December 7, 1941, a radar operator at the Opana radar station on Kahuku Point on the northern tip of the Hawaiian island of Oahu radioed the U.S. Army operations center at Fort Shafter. An army lieutenant in training there read the report. The radar operator wrote that "the biggest sightings" he'd ever seen, 50 or so airplanes, were on a course for Oahu. By now, the planes were about 70 miles (113 km) away. The army lieutenant believed the radar operator had picked up American B-17 bombers heading from California to Hawaii. For security reasons, he could not tell this to the radar operator. All he said was, "Well, don't worry about it." The lieutenant had made a big mistake. The radar operator had detected the advancing planes of an imminent Japanese sneak attack.

At 7:55 A.M., the first of two waves of Japanese fighters and bombers attacked the U.S. Navy port of Pearl Harbor and military airfields around it. About an hour later, a second wave completed the assault on Battleship Row. All told, approximately 360 Japanese warplanes attacked. The entire attack took less than two hours. The results were staggering.

The battleships *Arizona*, *California*, *West Virginia*, and *Oklahoma* were either blown up or sunk. The battleships *Nevada*, *Pennsylvania*, *Tennessee*, and *Maryland* were damaged. Eleven other

✛ One of the U.S. Navy ships sinks in the attack on Pearl Harbor.

ships were sunk or damaged, 188 aircraft were destroyed, and 159 aircraft were damaged. Casualties included approximately 2,400 dead and an estimated 1,200 wounded. Of the dead, more than 1,100 were aboard the *Arizona* when it exploded and sank.

MEANWHILE IN EUROPE

In December 1941, the Soviet army launches its counter-offensive against the German army near Moscow.

On the following morning, President Roosevelt addressed the nation. In his speech, he remarked that December 7, 1941, was "a date which will live in infamy." The reason for that statement was that the Japanese ambassador did not deliver his country's declaration of war until after Pearl Harbor was under attack. Roosevelt asked Congress to declare war on Japan. Two days later, keeping their pact with Japan, Germany and Italy declared war on the United States as well.

THE JAPANESE TIDE OF CONQUEST

When the Japanese fleet attacked Pearl Harbor, it was the first move in a 4,000-mile-wide (6,437 km) Japanese blitzkrieg that stretched from Wake Island in the Central Pacific to Burma on the border with India. ("Blitzkreig" is the German word for "lightning war.")

Wake Island is a small but important way station for U.S. aircraft traveling between Pearl Harbor and the Philippines. On December 8, about 450 marines and a marine fighter squadron were defending Wake Island. As the Japanese approached, marine gunners sank two destroyers and damaged a transport. The Japanese retreated, only to return two days later with reinforcements that would ultimately overpower the Marines.

Also on December 8, Japanese forces attacked the larger island of Guam. Because of a 1922 treaty with Japan, the United States had not

JAPAN'S ASSAULT

The Japanese attacked so many places so quickly—and conquered them all—because they hoped the shock of their victories would cause the Americans to quickly make peace. Here is the list of places and the dates on which the Japanese attacked.

Dec. 7, 1941:	Pearl Harbor
Dec. 8, 1941:	Wake Island The Philippines Malaya Hong Kong Thailand Guam
Dec. 24, 1941:	Netherlands East Indies
Jan. 15, 1942:	Burma
Jan. 23, 1942:	New Guinea
Jan. 31, 1942:	Singapore

been allowed to fortify the island. The small marine garrison had no chance of winning against the overwhelming Japanese force. The Japanese quickly took Guam.

The Japanese also attacked the Philippines, an island nation in the Pacific Ocean under U.S. guardianship at the time. Because the Philippines is west of the International Date Line, it is one day ahead of Hawaii, which is on the east side. So when Pearl Harbor was attacked on December 7, it was December 8 in the Philippines. The islands were under the command of U.S. General Douglas MacArthur. After destroying the American air force, Japanese troops landed on the northernmost island of Luzon and headed for the capital of Manila. By January 2, Manila had fallen and American and Filipino troops were retreating to the Bataan peninsula east of Manila. President Roosevelt ordered MacArthur to escape to Australia, not wanting to risk letting the valuable general fall into enemy hands. After a successful exit, MacArthur met the press in Australia and uttered the famous words "I came through, and I shall return." This was his vow that the Philippines would be liberated.

Lieutenant General Jonathan Wainwright took over for MacArthur in the Philippines. After Bataan fell, he and his troops held out on the island of Corregidor at the mouth of Manila Bay. On May 6, 1942, Wainwright's troops, out of food and ammunition, sick and tired, surrendered. Some troops scattered throughout the islands, refused to surrender, and carried out guerrilla warfare against the Japanese.

Even though it was impossible for America to send additional troops and supplies to the Philippines in early 1942, its loss was a crushing blow. All told, more than 70,000 troops from Bataan and

General Douglas MacArthur (right) shakes hands with Secretary of War Robert Patterson in New Guinea.

Corregidor surrendered. Only when the Philippines were liberated in 1944–45 did America discover what had happened to the troops on Bataan who had been forced to walk to POW (prisoner of war) camps north of Manila. During the approximately 60-mile (97 km) trek, the Imperial Japanese troops committed terrible atrocities against the prisoners. Estimates vary, but at least 10,000 and possibly 20,000 men died during what came to be called the Bataan Death March.

✠ In this 1943 photo we get an aerial view of Wake Island as seen by U.S. Navy dive-bombers.

THE SINKING OF REPULSE AND PRINCE OF WALES

Malaysia, a British colony located on the Malay Peninsula at the tip of Indochina, between the Indian and Pacific Oceans, supplied half the world's rubber and a third of its tin. These essential materials were needed by Japan's industries in order to secure Japan's domination of Asia. An important British naval base was situated on the end of the Malay Peninsula at Singapore. By taking Singapore, the Japanese would control access to the Pacific from the west through the straits of Sumatra. The British claimed they had constructed the strongest naval base in the world. Their army was large and to help bolster the harbor's defenses was a small fleet that included the powerful new battleship HMS *Prince of Wales* and the heavy cruiser HMS *Repulse*. Unfortunately, no aircraft carrier had been sent to help, so the fleet depended on the small number of short-range land-based planes based around Singapore for aerial protection.

MEANWHILE IN EUROPE

On December 11, 1941, Germany and Italy declare war on the United States. The United States promptly issues its declaration of war on them.

When Admiral Sir Tom Phillips, commander of the Far Eastern Fleet based in Singapore, heard that the Japanese had landed north in Malaya (now known as Malaysia), he ordered Force Z, composed of the *Repulse,* the *Prince of Wales,* and four destroyers, to sail north and destroy the Japanese fleet protecting the landing site.

But Japanese planes, based at airfields near Saigon in French Indochina, intercepted Force Z before it could reach the Japanese fleet.

✛ The British battleship HMS *Prince of Wales*.

Because Force Z had maintained radio silence in a failed attempt to keep its presence secret, it did not have any aerial protection. Even though both ships had strong anti-aircraft defenses, they were not enough to protect against the combined attack of dive-bombers and torpedo planes. Both ships were sunk.

It was a devastating defeat to the British. Winston Churchill told Parliament, "In my whole experience I do not remember any naval blow so heavy or so painful."

THE SURRENDER OF SINGAPORE

The tragedy of the Malaysian campaign would come to a head in early 1942. By January 15, Singapore had been reinforced by British troops. British general Arthur Percival had about 85,000 troops to face Japan's General Tomoyuki Yamashita's force of 35,000 soldiers. The British had proclaimed that Singapore was the most heavily fortified port in the world. Unfortunately, the reality was different. The fixed defenses, including heavy artillery, were designed to repel attacks from the sea. Instead, the Japanese chose to attack by land, where the British defenses were vulnerable.

American Brewster Buffalo fighter planes fly over Malaya.

Yamashita's men advanced steadily down the Malay Peninsula toward Singapore. Counter-attacks by the British failed, and by February 11, 1942, reservoirs in the middle of the island, which supplied the town of Singapore with water, had fallen into Japanese hands.

Isolated, without any hope of reinforcements, and facing a severe water shortage for his soldiers and the civilian population of Singapore, General Percival personally led a small group carrying the British flag, the Union Jack, and the white flag of surrender. He believed that

MEANWHILE IN EUROPE

In January 1942, American forces arrive in Great Britain.

further resistance was useless and his best course was to capitulate, which he did on February 15, 1942.

Percival's Malaysian campaign was one of the greatest military blunders in British history. More than 85,000 British, Indian, and Australian troops and local volunteers surrendered to a Japanese force of about 30,000 men.

Percival was never forgiven for his disastrous handling of the campaign. Though he had a place of honor, along with General Wainright, at the Japanese surrender ceremony on the USS *Missouri* in September 1945, he was shunned and excluded from other British World War II victory celebrations and commemorations.

✛ Civilians in Singapore during the Japanese advance toward the city.

THE BATTLE OF THE JAVA SEA

After the United States, Britain, and the Netherlands cut oil exports to Japan in 1941, the Japanese found themselves in desperate need of petroleum. They decided that they had to seize the island of Borneo in the Netherlands East Indies (Indonesia), the site of plentiful oil fields. Japanese troops invaded Borneo in early February 1942. On February 27, 1942, the Allies assembled a flotilla (small fleet) of American, Australian, and Dutch cruisers and destroyers to combat the Japanese invasion. Late that day, the first in a series of naval engagements that came to be called the Battle of the Java Sea began.

HMS VERSUS USS

The initials in front of the name of a warship identify the country that the ship belongs to. A British ship has the letters "HMS," which means "His Majesty's Ship" or "Her Majesty's Ship," depending on whether the British monarch is a king or a queen. "USS" means "United States Ship."

The fighting lasted until March 1. When it was over, the Allied fleet had lost 12 ships, including five cruisers, six destroyers, and one sloop. Only four U.S. destroyers survived. Four Japanese ships were damaged, and two transport ships were sunk. The way was now open for the Japanese to complete their conquest of the Netherlands East Indies.

⊢ A scene of destruction on one of the islands in the Netherlands East Indies during the Battle of the Java Sea.

After Pearl Harbor, President Roosevelt had the support he needed to join the war. In order to keep that support, he would need victories. There were only a handful of men who could lead the charge, and Roosevelt chose them wisely. Before the end of the war, these men would be promoted to the new five-star rank created during World War II. In the navy, this rank was admiral of the fleet. In the army, this rank was general of the army.

Army Chief of Staff General George C. Marshall

A World War I veteran, Army Chief of Staff General George C. Marshall was the head of the War Department's War Plans Division and then deputy chief of staff from 1938 to 1939. The War Department was the predecessor of today's Department of Defense. In 1939, Marshall was selected by President Roosevelt to be army chief of staff, a post he held through 1945.

Highly regarded by his peers, leaders of the Roosevelt administration, and members of Congress, Marshall was in charge of getting the U.S. Army and Army Air Corps ready for war and then leading

✝ George C. Marshall

them throughout the war. Winston Churchill called him one of the most important organizers of the Allied victory.

Admiral Ernest J. King

A veteran of World War I, Ernest J. King was appointed to lead the Atlantic Fleet in 1941 during the period of steadily escalating tensions with Germany.

The attack on Pearl Harbor brought Admiral King to Washington, D.C., as Commander in Chief of the U.S. Fleet in December 1941. He also became Chief of Naval Operations in March 1942, making him the most powerful naval leader in U.S. history. He held both positions through the rest of World War II. King guided all the navy's plans and global operations.

Army Air Force General Henry H. Arnold

Taught to fly by the Wright brothers, Henry "Hap" Arnold, another veteran of World War I, had a reputation as a "bomber man," having encouraged the development of the B-17 Flying Fortress and B-24 Liberator four-engine planes. (The Air Force remained part of the Army until after World War II.)

Prior to and during World War II, he directed air activities for the nation's global war against Germany and Japan. Under his direction, the U.S. Army Air Force grew from 22,000 officers and men with 3,900 planes to nearly 2.5 million men and 75,000 aircraft.

✠ (from left to right): General Douglas MacArthur, President Franklin D. Roosevelt, and Admiral Chester Nimitz

Admiral Chester W. Nimitz

During World War I, Lieutenant Chester Nimitz was assigned to submarine duty, gaining a reputation as an expert in undersea warfare.

He was given the post of chief of the Bureau of Navigation in June 1939 and held it through the difficult years leading up to U.S. entry into World War II. In the wake of the Japanese attack on Pearl Harbor, Nimitz was ordered to take over the Pacific fleet. He commanded American forces in the Southeast, Central, and North Pacific during their long advance across the ocean to full victory in August 1945.

General Douglas MacArthur

General Douglas MacArthur, the charismatic and flamboyant son of a Civil War hero, commanded the U.S. Army in the Pacific theater of World War II. He was acclaimed for his island-hopping strategy, in which U.S. forces would bypass and isolate islands with strong Japanese garrisons (troops stationed at military posts) by attacking and conquering nearby weakly held islands. This strategy was used against Japan with great success.

After the attack on Pearl Harbor, MacArthur commanded the defense of the Philippines until March 1942, when President Roosevelt ordered him to leave for Australia, where he took command of Allied forces in the southwestern Pacific.

From Australia, he launched the New Guinea campaign and later directed the campaigns that led to the liberation of the Philippines. MacArthur accepted the surrender of Japan on the USS *Missouri* on September 2, 1945. He was then named commander of the Allied powers in Japan and, as military governor, directed the Allied occupation of Japan after the war.

BATTLE OF THE CORAL SEA

Seeking to further expand their conquests, the Japanese next decided to take over Port Moresby in New Guinea, off the northeast coast of Australia. Port Moresby was a strategic location that could be used as both a naval and an air base. With it, the Japanese could control the Coral Sea and limit Australia's involvement in the war, forcing the Allies to launch all strikes from Hawaii, an extremely long haul.

MEANWHILE IN THE UNITED STATES

In April 1942, Japanese Americans in the United States are ordered to move to special relocation centers.

After intercepting Japanese naval transmissions, the Americans realized that the Japanese were planning to take Port Moresby with a large naval force that included the fleet carriers *Shokaku* and *Zuikaku* and the light carrier *Shoho*. Admiral Nimitz sent the only carriers he had available, the *Yorktown* and the *Lexington*, along with 141 aircraft, 5 cruisers, and 11 destroyers, to defend the port.

On May 4, 1942, the Americans intercepted and attacked the Japanese naval forces. The Battle of the Coral Sea was the first battle in naval history in which enemy fleets never came within sight of each other. The battle was fought long-distance between fighters, dive-bombers, and torpedo bombers launched from aircraft carriers.

Dive-bombers from the *Lexington* stumbled on the Japanese carrier *Shoho* and sank it in 10 minutes. On May 8, 1942, the Japanese decided to postpone the attack on Port Moresby and instead try to take out the

Soldiers leap off the badly damaged USS *Lexington* shortly before it sinks in the Battle of the Coral Sea.

two American carriers. The Americans planned to do the same thing to the Japanese carriers. Both sides launched aircraft and inflicted damage on the other. The *Shokaku* was damaged and forced to retreat, and the *Lexington* was hit and finally destroyed by internal explosions.

The Americans lost the *Lexington* and 74 aircraft. The Japanese lost 80 aircraft and a small carrier, the *Shoho*, in addition to the damaged *Shokaku*. But the Americans had stopped the Japanese from invading Port Moresby and put one of Japan's carriers out of commission for several months. It was the first time the seemingly invincible Japanese had been stopped.

The Battle of the Coral Sea was a victory for Japan. Its fleet had inflicted greater losses on the Americans. But the battle was also a type of victory for the Americans for two reasons. The first reason was that the Americans had prevented the Japanese from capturing Port Moresby. Also, as a result of battle damage and aircraft losses, the Japanese fleet carriers *Shokaku* and *Zuikaku* could not be used in the upcoming Battle of Midway as originally planned.

CHINA-BURMA-INDIA THEATER: GENERAL STILWELL

The war in the China-Burma-India theater (CBI) was known as the "forgotten war." The reason was that CBI was last in line, after the needs of the European, Mediterranean, Pacific, and Southwest Pacific areas. Also, the battles received little publicity compared to those in other territories.

Allied leaders of CBI focused on the goals of keeping the Chinese army supplied, coordinating with the Chinese army an offensive to liberate Burma, and using China as a base of operations for air strikes against the Japanese. The tremendous physical fighting was matched only by the enormous behind-the-scenes political bickering between the countries involved.

The Americans and the British backed the Nationalist Chinese led by Chiang Kai-shek. They did little to help Chiang's rival, the Chinese Communist leader Mao Tse-tung. This was despite

A Japanese drawing entitled "Start of Burma Campaign, Japanese Tanks Advancing 1942."

╫ Joseph Stilwell

the fact that the Chinese Communists were generally more successful at fighting the Japanese than the Nationalist Chinese. The reason for this was that, unlike the Chinese Communists, the Nationalists suffered from low morale and corruption.

The United States had urged Chiang Kai-shek to appoint as his army chief of staff an American general named Joe Stilwell. Although fluent in Chinese and one of the best soldiers in the field, Stilwell was not exactly the ideal candidate for this job. Called "Vinegar Joe," Stilwell was talented, but abrasive and frequently argued with Chiang Kai-shek. He detested the Chinese leader's tolerance of corruption.

Despite the many problems, the Allies launched a series of attacks against Japanese forces in Burma, from 1942 to 1945. It was not until the summer of 1945 that Burma was retaken. Vinegar Joe wasn't there to see it though. In 1944, Chiang Kai-shek had him removed from his job and recalled to the states because of "irreconcilable differences."

THE BATTLE OF MIDWAY

In the spring of 1942, Japanese power was at its zenith. Though Japan had been checked in early May at the Battle of the Coral Sea, it had conquered virtually half the world.

The earlier shock in April 1942 of the Doolittle Raid, a U.S. Army Air Force bomber raid on the Japanese home islands, launched off the aircraft carrier USS *Hornet*, caused the Japanese high command to rethink things. They realized they needed to strengthen their defensive island perimeter in the Central Pacific and destroy the U.S. carriers once and for all.

✛ A Japanese cruiser is heavily damaged by U.S. Navy dive-bombers during the Battle of Midway.

The island they felt would accomplish both goals was American-held Midway, less than 1,200 miles (1,931 km) northwest of Pearl Harbor. What the Japanese did not know was that U.S. Navy intelligence had broken their code and knew their plans.

The Japanese leader of the battle was Admiral Isoroku Yamamoto, the man who had planned the attack on Pearl Harbor. He assembled a huge fleet of more than 160 ships. A small part of this fleet he sent north as a diversion. It would attack and capture the Alaskan islands of Attu and Kiska in the Aleutians.

But the main thrust was against Midway. For that, his primary strike force was a battle group assembled around the fleet carriers *Kaga*, *Akagi*, *Soryu*, and *Hiryu*.

Against the Japanese armada, Admiral Nimitz, the commander in chief in the Pacific, could assemble only two healthy carriers, the *Enterprise* and the *Hornet*. When the *Yorktown*, crippled in the Battle of the Coral Sea, sailed into Pearl Harbor, Nimitz was there to greet it. He had been told that it would take three months to repair the ship. Nimitz told the repair crews that they had three days. Three days later, the *Yorktown* was sailing off to battle.

The Battle of Midway was fought from June 4 to 7, 1942. When it was over, the outnumbered and outgunned U.S. fleet had delivered to Japan a decisive defeat. All four Japanese fleet carriers were sunk, along with one cruiser, and another cruiser was damaged. In addition, Japan lost more than 260 airplanes. American losses were heavy, too. The U.S. forces lost 147 aircraft and the *Yorktown* and had a destroyer sunk. But America was overjoyed. The Japanese had been stopped. The tide had finally turned.

U.S. Navy Yeoman Jack Adams was aboard the *Yorktown* for its final battle. Adams and his crewmates were forced to abandon ship in a life raft as the ship was hit with torpedoes and dive-bombers. It was only later that he discovered the results of the battle he had fought to win.

We learned that four of the enemy carriers had been sunk along with the heavy cruiser. The Japanese lost all their planes and most of their aircrew, either in combat or for sheer lack of a place to land. It was sad to hear that Yorktown *sank after the heroic efforts of Captain Buckmaster and his salvage team. The air groups on all three of our carriers also took a beating, particularly the torpedo squadrons. However, this was the victory we needed.*

GLOSSARY

Allies—The name for the nations, primarily Great Britain, the United States, the Soviet Union, and France, united against the Axis powers.

Armada—A large group of warships.

Axis—The countries, primarily Germany, Italy, and Japan, that fought against the Allies.

Blitzkrieg—The German word for "lightning war." A swift, overpowering military offensive of combined land and air forces led by tanks and other armored vehicles.

Campaign—A series of major military operations designed to achieve a long-range goal.

Garrison—A military post or a group of troops stationed at a particular location.

Isolationists—Those who advocate that their country remain aloof from political or economic relationships with other countries, especially ones at war.

League of Nations—A world organization of nations established in 1920 for the purpose of peacefully promoting diplomatic relations and commerce. It was dissolved in 1946 and replaced by the United Nations.

Nazi—The acronym for NAtionalsoZIalist, the first word of the official title of Hitler's political party, the Nationalsozialistische Deutsche Arbeiterpartie or NSDAP (National Socialist German Workers' Party).

Soviet Union—From 1917–1991, the nation known officially as the Union of Soviet Socialist Republics; a nation containing 15 communist-governed republics and dominated by its largest republic, Russia.

Treaty—A formal agreement between two or more nations that contains terms of trade, military alliance, or other points of mutual interest.

Treaty of Washington—An agreement signed by the United States, Great Britain, France, Italy, and Japan in Washington, D.C., on February 6, 1922, that attempted to limit the growth of naval warship construction. The United States and Great Britain were allowed to construct the most ships, then came Japan, followed by France and Italy.

Tripartite Pact—The treaty between Germany, Italy, and Japan intended to provide mutual assistance in the event of an attack on any of them by the United States.

INDEX

Allied powers, 4–6
in World War I, 10
Allied powers in Japan, 39
Anschluss, of Germany
with Austria, 17
"Arsenal of Democracy"
speech, 18–20
Atlantic Charter, 23
Atomic bombs, at World
War II conclusion, 6
Attu, invasion of, 44
Australia, 9, 40
Battle of the Java Sea, 34
MacArthur's escape to, 28,
39
Austria
Anschluss with Germany,
17
in World War I, 10
Axis powers, 4–6, 17, 20
B-17 Flying Fortress, 24,
37
B-24 Liberator, 37
Bataan Death March, 29
Blitzkrieg, Japanese, 27
Burma, 27, 42, 43
Central Powers, in World
War I, 10
Chiang Kai-shek, 6–7, 14
in China-Burma-India
Theater, 42–43
China, 4–6
in China-Burma-India
Theater, 42–43
civil war in, 14
Communists in, 14, 43
Japanese occupation of,
14–15, 22
Republic of, 15
China-Burma-India (CBI)
Theater, 42–43
Churchill, Winston S., 6
George Marshall and, 36
meeting with Roosevelt, 23

on sinking of *Repulse* and
Prince of Wales, 31
Civil war, in China, 14
Communist Party, in China,
15, 43
Coral Sea, Battle of,
40–41, 44
Corregidor, Japanese
attack on, 28–29
Council of Ten, World War I
and, 10
Dive-bombers, 29
in Battle of Midway, 44–45
in Battle of the Coral Sea,
40
Doolittle Raid, 44
Europe, 4, 6, 8, 21, 23, 26,
30, 33
rise of Hitler in, 16
Fascism, 4, 17
Fireside Chats, 18–21
Force Z, in Malaya, 30–31
"Forgotten war," 42
"Four Freedoms" speech,
20–21
French Indochina, Japanese
occupation of, 17, 22,
30–31
Germany, 4, 6, 18
Anschluss with Austria, 16
conquests by (map), 8
declares war on United
States, 26
"Hap" Arnold versus, 37
invasion of Soviet Union
by, 23
London air raids by, 21
in Pact of Steel, 17
siege of Leningrad by, 23
Soviet counteroffensive
versus, 26
after World War I, 13
in World War I, 10
Great Britain, 4–6, 10

in Battle of the Java Sea,
34
in China-Burma-India
Theater, 42–43
Japan versus, 30–31,
32–33
United States and, 33
Washington Naval
Conference Treaty, 13
in World War I, 10
Hitler, Adolf, 4–5, 16
Indochina, 30
Japanese occupation of,
17, 22, 30–31
International Date Line, 28
Island-hopping, 39
Isolationists, 18
Italy, 4, 6, 10, 18
declares war on United
States, 26
in Pact of Steel, 17
after World War I, 13
in World War I, 10
Japan, 4, 6, 10, 18
attack on Pearl Harbor by,
24–26
in Battle of Midway,
44–45
in Battle of the Coral Sea,
40–41
in Battle of the Java Sea,
34
in China-Burma-India
theater, 42–43
Great Britain versus,
30–31, 32–33
"Hap" Arnold versus, 37
invasion of China by,
14–15
oil required by, 34–35
prisoner-of-war atrocities
by, 29
rise of military government
in, 10–13